Mastering Disagreements
Strategies for Effective Conflict Resolution

Bertram A. Hunter

Table of Contents

1. Introduction 2
2. Understanding Disagreements and Conflicts: A Deeper Dive 3
   - 2.1. The Nature of Disagreements: A Focal Point 3
   - 2.2. Scanning Conflicts: The Dark Side of Disagreeing 4
   - 2.3. Tracing the Roots: Where Do Disagreements and Conflicts Originate? 4
   - 2.4. Bridging the Divide: The Importance of Conflict Resolution ... 5
3. The Psychology of Disagreements: Why do they Happen? 7
   - 3.1. The Sociological and Psychological Underpinnings 7
   - 3.2. Cognitive Biases: Fueling Disagreements 8
   - 3.3. Emotional Intelligence and Disagreements 8
4. Listening with Empathy: A Key to Conflict Resolution 10
   - 4.1. The Concept of Empathy 10
   - 4.2. The Essence of Listening with Empathy 11
   - 4.3. Triune of Empathetic Listening: The Three Levels 11
   - 4.4. Practicing Empathy: A How-To Guide 12
   - 4.5. Empathy and Conflict Resolution: Two Peas in a Pod 12
5. Assertiveness vs Aggressiveness: Make Your Point without Making an Enemy 14
   - 5.1. Understanding Assertiveness 14
   - 5.2. Assertiveness and Its Importances 15
   - 5.3. Assertiveness vs Aggressiveness 15
   - 5.4. The Art of Assertiveness 16
   - 5.5. When Assertiveness Becomes Aggression 16
   - 5.6. Conclusion 17
6. Effective Communication: Say What You Mean & Understand Others 18
   - 6.1. Understanding Effective Communication 18

 6.2. The Power of Clear Expression 18
 6.3. Improving Expression: Strategies and Techniques 19
 6.4. The Importance of Understanding Others 19
 6.5. Developing Understanding: Strategies and Techniques 20
7. Emotionally Intelligent Responses: Navigating Disagreements Without Escalating Them 21
 7.1. Emotional Intelligence: A Primer 21
 7.2. The Impact of Emotional Intelligence in Conflict Resolution . 22
 7.3. Techniques for Utilizing Emotional Intelligence 22
 7.4. Emotional Intelligence: Keys to Success 23
8. Building Cooperation: Collaborative Techniques for Resolving Disputes 25
 8.1. The Importance of Building Cooperation 25
 8.2. Understanding the Principles of Cooperation 26
 8.3. The Role of Communication in Building Cooperation 26
 8.4. Collaborative Techniques for Resolving Disputes 27
 8.5. The Path Forward: Turning Principles into Practice 27
9. Negotiation Skills: Finding Common Ground 29
 9.1. Understanding the Terrain 29
 9.2. Building Bridges Not Walls 30
 9.3. Communicate, Don't Confront 30
 9.4. Finding the Common Ground 31
 9.5. Conclusion 31
10. Addressing and Resolving Conflicts: Tools and Techniques 32
 10.1. Problem Identification: The First Step 32
 10.2. Active Listening: A Tool for Understanding 33
 10.3. Open Communication: The Bridge to Resolution 33
 10.4. Conflict Styles: Understanding Your Approach 34
 10.5. Negotiation: The Art of Agreement 34
 10.6. Forgiveness and Reconciliation: The Final Steps 35

11. Maintaining Relationships Post-Conflict: Paving Way for
Forgiveness and Growth 36
    11.1. The Essence of Forgiveness 36
    11.2. Reconciliation and Healing 37
    11.3. Paving the Path for Post-Conflict Growth 37

Peace is not absence of conflict, it is the ability to handle conflict by peaceful means.

— Ronald Reagan

Chapter 1. Introduction

Master disagreements like never before with our Special Report, "Mastering Disagreements: Strategies for Effective Conflict Resolution." This riveting report doesn't merely dictate theory; it captivates readers by imparting practical, actionable skills that you can apply in both professional and personal settings. Relationships can be a complex dance of opinions, and it's inevitable to step on some toes on occasion. When disagreements arise, they don't have to spiral into full-blown conflicts. And here comes the best part! This report could be your golden ticket to learning how to navigate these tricky situations with grace and ease, ensuring lasting, respectful relationships. Purchase our Special Report today, and come on a game-changing journey to transform the way you approach, manage, and resolve disagreements. You're not just buying a report, you are investing in lifelong skills for tranquil conflict resolution. Be steered by knowledge, empowered by confidence - grab your copy now!

Chapter 2. Understanding Disagreements and Conflicts: A Deeper Dive

The world is bursting with an incredible diversity of people, each brimming with their unique perceptions, beliefs, and values. These work as navigational aid, leading individuals along their life paths. But in this grand journey of life, it's inevitable that these paths cross, creating an intersection of thoughts, a symphony of varying viewpoints. It's at this junction where disagreements are born, but do they always have to lead to discord? This comprehensive exploration seeks to unravel the fundamental dynamics of disagreement and conflict, enabling a better understanding and providing a first step towards effective resolution.

2.1. The Nature of Disagreements: A Focal Point

Disagreements may seem inherently negative, an embodiment of conflict. However, it's important to dispel this myth. A disagreement is simply a divergence in viewpoints, a natural consequence of the astonishing diversity we find in human thinking and perception. Two individuals, with their exclusive life experiences and belief systems, will not always align perfectly on every issue - whether it's about deciding on a business strategy, choosing a weekend outing, or debating a topic of global importance. But rather than becoming a hindrance, these disparities can be fuel for growth, stimulating lively discussions and fostering creative solutions.

On workplace scale, disagreements may highlight unseen issues, can prompt innovative ideas, or could stoke a much-needed shakeup to routine, driving the organization toward higher efficiency and productivity. In personal relationships, they can offer deeper insights into each other's perspectives, enriching the relationship with understanding and empathy. The key is to respect these differences and channelize them constructively.

2.2. Scanning Conflicts: The Dark Side of Disagreeing

While disagreements are fundamentally neutral, the line between a healthy disagreement and a harmful conflict often blurs. A disagreement slips into conflict territory when it is accompanied by escalating emotional intensity, stubbornness, retaliation, or outright hostility. When mishandled, disagreements become persisting issues, and the opportunity for growth morphs into the prospect of disrupted relationships or work environments.

Conflicts frequently start small, a spark that can be easily extinguished, but when neglected or mismanaged, they can grow into infernos that consume all in their destructive path. At a personal level, unresolved conflicts can lead to stress, discontentment, an unhealthy ambiance at home, and at times, even complete severance of relationships. Similarly, in a professional context, conflicts may hinder productivity, reduce morale of the workforce, promote politics, and if continues, could even jeopardize the organization's success.

2.3. Tracing the Roots: Where Do Disagreements and Conflicts Originate?

Let's take a step back and delve into the origins of disagreements. They stem from differences, differences in perspectives, beliefs, values, and desires. As humans, we all perceive the world with our distinctive lens, and each of our lenses is tinted with the color of our unique experiences.

When these perceptions clash over a particular issue, a disagreement emerges. For instance, we might differ on political views based on our inherent biases, or we might have a conflicting opinion about a business proposal, influenced by our individual understanding and insight.

Similarly, conflicts often originate from communication breakdown, misinterpreted intentions, unfair treatment, competitiveness, or unmet needs. They may crop up within family dynamics over inheritance or within a team at work over a promotional opportunity.

2.4. Bridging the Divide: The Importance of Conflict Resolution

Clearly, disagreements and conflicts are inevitable parts of our lives, both personally and professionally. But rather than viewing them as stumbling blocks, it would serve us to see them as stepping stones towards attainment of better understanding, stronger relationships and successful collaborations.

This necessitates mastery of conflict resolution strategies, for unresolved conflicts are not merely static problems. Like a rolling stone, they gather more issues and emotional intensity, growing larger and more complex with time. Effective conflict resolution involves identifying and addressing these disagreements and conflicts at an early stage, ensuring that they do not fester into bigger issues.

Practicing conflict resolution can greatly enhance your interpersonal relationships and can create a harmonious environment. Enhanced productivity at workplaces, reduced stress, and increased understanding in personal relationships are just a few of the myriad benefits that you can reap.

The recognition that divergence of viewpoints is inevitable and natural is the first step towards effective conflict resolution. As we delve deeper into the roots of disagreement and conflict, and unearth their causes and true nature, we become better equipped to address and manage them. And this begins our journey towards a more harmonious and understanding world. In the forthcoming chapters of this walk through conflict resolution, we will offer effective strategies, tools, and techniques to successfully navigate through the narrow path of disagreements, without stepping on anyone's toes, metaphorically, of course.

Chapter 3. The Psychology of Disagreements: Why do they Happen?

From the dawn of human existence, disagreements have been central to our interactions with others. They are threaded into every conversation, debate, negotiation, and argument we partake in. Understanding the psychology behind disagreements and why they occur is the cornerstone of mastering conflict resolution.

3.1. The Sociological and Psychological Underpinnings

Human beings are social animals with unique personalities, perspectives, and experiences. It's this diversity that lays the groundwork for disagreements. We don't always see eye-to-eye, and this divergence in thought forms the central tenet of disagreements.

Sociologically, we frequently identify with different social groups, each with its own norms, practices, and values that shape our perspectives. A person's upbringing, cultural background, religious beliefs, education, and even employment can guide their thought processes.

Meanwhile, from the psychological standpoint, our personal beliefs, attitudes, and cognitive biases can greatly influence how we perceive and interpret stimuli, thus shaping our opinions. Over time, our experiences catalyze the formation of mental models, cognitive schemas, or "blueprints" that help us process information. When confronted with viewpoints that challenge these deeply ingrained schemas, we are inclined to sway away, leading to disagreements.

3.2. Cognitive Biases: Fueling Disagreements

Cognitive biases are systematic errors in thinking that can cloud our judgment and decision-making skills. They can create fertile ground for disagreements as they often lead us to misinterpret information.

There are many types of cognitive biases that can trigger disagreements, such as:

1. Confirmation Bias: We tend to favor information that aligns with our existing beliefs or values, and often discard evidence to the contrary. This can lead to stubbornness and fewer compromises in the face of disagreements.
2. The Fundamental Attribution Error: We have a tendency to attribute our own actions to external circumstances, while attributing others' actions to their inner characteristics. This can lead to misunderstandings and thus disagreements.
3. The False consensus effect: We overestimate how much others share our beliefs and values. When we realize this isn't the case, disputes can ensue.
4. The Backfire Effect: When confronted with information that challenges our deeply held beliefs, we tend to believe in our original stance even more strongly.

Recognizing these cognitive biases in ourselves and others is a crucial step towards overcoming disagreements.

3.3. Emotional Intelligence and Disagreements

Emotional intelligence refers to the ability to understand, use, and manage emotions in positive ways to communicate effectively, overcome challenges, and defuse conflict. High emotional intelligence can often mean better management of disagreements.

Individuals who possess high emotional intelligence are generally more self-aware. They can recognize their emotions and how these feelings affect their interactions. They're also better at managing their responses, enabling them to deal with provocation without escalating into a full-blown dispute.

Equipped with empathy, they can understand and share the feelings of others, putting them in an excellent position to navigate through the rocky terrains of disagreements. They're also good at gauging social dynamics, enabling them to predict potential conflict areas, facilitating proactive resolution.

Understanding the psychology behind disagreements isn't the end game, but it gives us a solid foundation to build upon. By recognizing these complexities, we're better equipped to approach disagreements with a strategic and open-minded approach that favors resolution over escalation.

Chapter 4. Listening with Empathy: A Key to Conflict Resolution

The process of conflict resolution is like a two-sided coin. On one side lies the urge and necessity to express and validate oneself; and on the other side lies the ability to comprehend and respect other's perspectives, ideas, and feelings. And this is where the inherent power of empathy kicks in.

4.1. The Concept of Empathy

Empathy, as a concept, can be described as the capacity to comprehend or feel what another person is experiencing from within their frame of reference. Put it simply, it's the ability to put oneself in another's shoes. However, the application of empathy is much more profound and complex, especially in conflict resolution.

The applicability of empathy as a tool for conflict resolution is based on the core understanding that conflicts or disagreements occur when there is a perceived threat to an individual's needs, interests, or concerns. According to the American psychologist, Dr. Carl Rogers, empathetic listening is a vital precursor to compassion, and consequently, to conflict resolution.

Empathy allows one to understand these needs or concerns at a deeper level, providing an avenue for deescalating the conflict and fostering connection and understanding.

4.2. The Essence of Listening with Empathy

Listening with empathy is more than just hearing the words that another person is saying. It demands an emotional engagement, an intellectual involvement, and a level of patience that can facilitate the understanding of the other party's emotional state. It's not merely a receptive skill but an active process.

The process involves a focus not only on words but also on non-verbal cues such as body language and tone of voice. It's about detecting the feelings behind the words and showing an understanding of the other person's perspective – whether we agree with it or not.

Empathetic listening also involves the courage to bear witness to another person's raw emotions and vulnerabilities - something that can be both uncomfortable and potentially transformative.

4.3. Triune of Empathetic Listening: The Three Levels

Empathetic listening can be conceptualized into three different, yet co-dependent, levels:

1. Recognition – The initial level of empathetic listening is the recognition of the other person's feelings and sentiments. Truly grasp what is being expressed, both verbally and non-verbally.
2. Understanding – This level involves the comprehension of the reasons or circumstances that have led to these feelings. Delve deeper into why these emotions were invoked.
3. Responsive – The final level involves the communication of this understanding back to the person. Echo the sentiments conveyed

to assert them, and provide a response, if needed.

This triune combination helps create a safe and understanding space where both parties can express, validate, and comprehend each other sentiments, paving the way to a harmonious resolution.

4.4. Practicing Empathy: A How-To Guide

The road to mastering empathetic listening can be intimidating and challenging, as it requires self-awareness, patience, and practice. But the rewards, in terms of personally rewarding relationships and effective conflict resolution, can be unquantifiably vast.

Start by being fully present in your conversations. Give undivided attention. Show active involvement by responding, nodding, or with facial expressions.

Secondly, approach the conversation with an open mind. Keep aside preconceived notions or judgments about the other person or situation. The intention should be understanding the other party, not proving oneself right.

Moreover, try to understand the emotion behind the words. Watch out for non-verbal cues like body language, tone of voice, etc.

Lastly, validate their feelings. Assure them that their feelings matter. Even if you disagree, stay respectful and considerate. Post understanding, communicate that back to the other person.

4.5. Empathy and Conflict Resolution: Two Peas in a Pod

The application of empathy stands paramount in conflict resolution.

Through empathetic listening, one can get to the crux of disagreements – the fear, the feelings, the unexpressed sentiments. This understanding aids in addressing and resolving the root cause of the conflict, rather than merely scratching the surface level issues.

It also sets the stage for effective communication. When one feels heard and understood, they are generally more open to hearing and understanding your perspective. This reciprocative environment fosters mutual respect and compromise, allowing conflicts to be resolved in a way that is much more satisfactory to both parties.

In closing, one can say, listening with empathy is not just hearing another's words, it's about understanding the music behind them. When we endeavor to understand the melodies that ring in another's heart, we are bridging chasms, connecting at a deeper level, and resolving conflicts in a much more harmonious and gratifying manner. Embrace the power of empathy. Transform the way you approach disagreements and conflicts. Unearth the potential of a harmonious co-existence.

Chapter 5. Assertiveness vs Aggressiveness: Make Your Point without Making an Enemy

Are you struggling to express your thoughts unhesitatingly, or do you sometimes wonder if your assertiveness might be perceived as aggression? As you navigate this nuanced territory, you'll find this chapter offering practical and theoretical insights that will transform your communication skills, providing you with the tools to make your point assertively, without appearing abrasive.

5.1. Understanding Assertiveness

Assertiveness, at its core, is the ability to communicate your thoughts, feelings, and needs assertively and respectfully. It is about standing up for yourself, but doing so in a way that also respects the rights and dignity of others. Assertiveness is a healthy communication style that involves expressing your needs, wants, and feelings in an open, honest, and direct manner. It does not seek to dominate others, rather it's grounded in mutual respect.

Contrarily, many people equate being assertive with being aggressive, but there is a fundamental difference between the two. Aggression typically involves intimidation, disregarding others' feelings, and often leads to violating others' rights. Aggression tends to be domineering and singularly focused on personal wants and desires, generally at the expense of others.

These two communication styles couldn't be more different in both their approach and their outcomes. However, understanding the difference between them can sometimes be blurry, leading to misconceptions and misunderstandings.

5.2. Assertiveness and Its Importances

Assertiveness focuses primarily on healthy communication, which is built on the premise of respect. This communication style values both the speaker's and the listener's rights, ensuring that neither party is disregarded or disrespected. Assertiveness is fundamentally about balance, seeking to promote equality within communication. This is not only beneficial for individuals, but also enormously advantageous for fostering healthier personal relationships and more productive work environments.

Moreover, assertiveness can greatly impact your self-esteem and confidence. When you practice speaking your mind in a respectful way, you affirm your self-worth and build your self-confidence. It has been seen to reduce anxiety and stress, paving the way to a mentally healthier you. You increase your chances of getting your needs met, avoid feeling victimized, and enjoy better relationships overall. .

5.3. Assertiveness vs Aggressiveness

Aggressiveness can get easily misinterpreted as assertiveness in a world where self-expression and persuasive articulation are idealized. This can lead to relationships getting strained and an unhealthy, hostile environment setting in. In contrast, assertiveness, when used correctly, bolstered relationships, making them healthier and more balanced. The key distinction lies in the impact each type of communication has on others in terms of respect, personal boundaries, and consent.

For instance, aggressive behavior typically manipulates, controls, or undermines others. It lacks consideration for other people's rights and boundaries. It often escalates conflict, creates resistance, and fosters resentment. It may give you a temporary sense of control and satisfaction, but in the long run, it erodes relationships and generates negativity.

On the other hand, assertive behavior shows a high level of respect for all parties involved. It acknowledges differences of opinion, allows for compromise, and facilitates solution-focused discussions. It empowers the individual to express their own needs while also considering the needs of others. This fosters mutual understanding and respect, promoting healthier and more productive interactions.

5.4. The Art of Assertiveness

Learning to be assertive is an art and a craft that anyone can develop with practice, patience, and commitment. It is about learning to express your feelings and thoughts clearly, concisely, and directly, yet respectfully.

Here are some strategies that can help:

Practice consistency. Consistency breeds credibility, so stand by your words and do what you've said.

Remember, it is perseverance and an openness to continually hone these skills that will lead to transformative results. No one becomes an assertive communicator overnight, but with practice, you are bound to see a progressive improvement in your interaction skills, leading the way for more balanced, respectful relationships.

5.5. When Assertiveness Becomes Aggression

Understanding the relationship between assertiveness and aggression is key to successfully navigating communication challenges. While it's true that assertiveness can transform into aggression if it disregards the rights of others, recognizing the signs will prevent slipping into an aggressive communication style.

If you find yourself resorting to dismissive or belittling language, employing threats, or utilizing passive-aggressive methods in your communication, it's time to step back and reassess. These can often lead to a vicious cycle of resentment and strained relationships.

Be mindful of your tone, language, and body language. Respect is crucial in all interactions, and embracing a respectful tone, choosing your words wisely, and maintaining open and non-threatening body language can go a long way to avoid misunderstanding and enhance effective assertive communication.

5.6. Conclusion

Assertiveness is not about winning or losing; it's about establishing an equilibrium of rights and respect. Recognizing the difference between assertiveness and aggression is invaluable. Aggression can foster a toxic atmosphere and damage relationships. Conversely, assertiveness cultivates healthier interactions and builds stronger relationships based on mutual understanding and respect. It's a nurturing soil, not just for you but also for those around you. Remember, being assertive is a skill; it can be learned and improved with practice.

Adopting an assertive communication style can indeed be a powerful tool for conflict resolution. It upholds your rights while respecting those of others, thus paving the way for healthier, more respectful, and balanced relationships. So, embark on this journey of learning the nuances of assertiveness, and watch as it transmutes your personal and professional encounters, making them more enriching and fulfilling.

Chapter 6. Effective Communication: Say What You Mean & Understand Others

Effective communication is central to any relationship—personal or professional. The primary facets of this component are expressing one's thoughts and ideas clearly and understanding the perspectives of others. Let's embark on this journey to master the art of communication.

6.1. Understanding Effective Communication

Understanding effective communication starts with the comprehension of two vital aspects: saying what you mean and understanding others. The former pertains to our ability to articulate thoughts, feelings, and perspectives in a manner that doesn't harm or offend others. The latter, on the other hand, relates to our capacity to grasp the concept being conveyed to us. In essence, effective communication is about balance—articulation and comprehension working in harmony.

6.2. The Power of Clear Expression

What we express and how we express it can significantly affect the outcome of any conversation, especially when disagreements are in play. Cultivating a knack for clear expression fosters understanding and minimizes copious potential misunderstandings or misinterpretations. Moreover, clear expression aids in establishing credibility and fostering trust within relationships, essential ingredients for constructive dialogue.

6.3. Improving Expression: Strategies and Techniques

There are several strategies to enhance clarity of expression:

1. Always be clear and concise: Stick to the point and avoid unnecessary surplus information that might muddle your main message.
2. Employ the right tone and body language: Non-verbal cues often speak louder than words. Convey your message properly using a respectful tone and positive body language.
3. Use understandable language: Jargon may cause confusion, particularly when the listener is unfamiliar with them. Prefer common, understandable language over technical terminology.
4. Practice active listening: To gauge if your points are being understood, listening actively to the responses of others is crucial. This will also give you cues for modifying your communication style, if needed.

6.4. The Importance of Understanding Others

Just as important as conveying your thoughts clearly is the ability to understand others. Accurate comprehension fosters a sense of respect and empathy, propelling you towards amicable conflict resolution.

6.5. Developing Understanding: Strategies and Techniques

Here are some proven strategies to enhance your understanding of others' viewpoints:

1. Practice active listening: Pay full attention to the speaker, showing interest through nonverbal cues like nodding or maintaining eye contact.
2. Seek clarification: If a point is unclear, ask the speaker to elaborate. Don't assume or interpret things based on half-baked understanding.
3. Be open-minded: Let go of biases and preconceptions. Entertain the possibility that there exists an alternative viewpoint that may be just as valid as yours.
4. Reflect on what's been said: Taking time to contemplate the speaker's point of view can significantly enhance your understanding and possibly reveal new perspectives that were previously overlooked.

Effective communication, in essence, is a two-sided coin. On the one side lies clear, concise articulation, and on the other, respectful understanding of others. By mastering both sides of this coin, you can navigate even the most heated disagreements with grace and efficacy, fostering an atmosphere of mutual respect and understanding.

Chapter 7. Emotionally Intelligent Responses: Navigating Disagreements Without Escalating Them

Mastering the art of emotionally intelligent responses is a crucial part of navigating disagreements without escalating them into full-blown conflicts. This segment of our report delves into the theoretical underpinning of emotional intelligence, the practical implications, and diversely applicable techniques that you can utilize in multiple settings to keep tensions from flaring and relationships from faltering. Keeping disagreements contained is an adept maneuver, and you can accomplish this by adapting your responses to be emotionally intelligent.

7.1. Emotional Intelligence: A Primer

Our journey through emotionally intelligent responses must commence with a robust understanding of emotional intelligence. Emotional intelligence, often termed as EQ (Emotional Quotient), refers to a person's capability to recognize, comprehend, utilize, and manage both their emotions and the emotions of others in an effective and constructive manner. This capacity includes skills such as emotional awareness, the ability to harness emotions and apply them to tasks such as brainstorming and resolving problems, and the ability to manage emotions, including controlling our own and soothing others'.

EQ plays a significant role in how we interact, communicate, empathize and negotiate with others. It greatly affects our professional and personal relationships, distinguishing between fruitful alliances and tumultuous, chaotic encounters. Therefore, to navigate disagreements without escalating them, it is imperative to respond with an emotionally intelligent mindset.

7.2. The Impact of Emotional Intelligence in Conflict Resolution

Now that we've unraveled the fabric of emotional intelligence let's explore how it intertwines with conflict resolution.

Emotionally Intelligent responses in difficult situations often determine whether a disagreement escalates into a severe conflict or resolves amicably. Taking a step back to see things from the other person's perspective, exercising empathy, utilizing active listening skills, and communicating your point of view without attacking the other party can profoundly impact the trajectory of an argument. EQ permits us to preserve dignity, respect, and integrity in our interactions, even during disputes, which are critical determinants in maintaining healthy relationships long term.

Although emotions often run high in disagreements, responding rather than reacting allows individuals to maintain control over the situation and steer it towards a resolution. Emotionally intelligent responses – calm, composed, considerate – make it easier to negotiate, compromise, and find a middle ground. They create an environment conducive to open, honest, and constructive dialogue.

7.3. Techniques for Utilizing Emotional Intelligence

Now that we've established emotional intelligence's significance and contribution to conflict resolution, we shall delve into practical methods to hone these skills.

1. **Mindful Self-awareness**: Becoming marginally more self-aware can greatly enhance your ability to manage disputes. Recognizing your triggers, understanding your emotional reaction patterns, and acknowledging how they impact others can prevent impulsive, ill-thought actions and responses that can aggravate a situation.

2. **Empathetic Listening**: Practicing empathetic listening allows you to appreciate and understand another individual's perspective, detering the escalation of disagreements. Empathy involves suspending your own frame of reference and assumptions to fully understand and appreciate another person's viewpoint.

3. **Non-verbal Communication**: Understanding and effectively using non-verbal communication can also play a significant role in managing disagreements. Body language, tone of voice, and facial expressions impact the received message. Paying attention to these can avoid misunderstandings and show the other person that you are invested in resolving the conflict.

4. **Proactive Approach**: Proactively recognizing potential disagreements and addressing issues before they escalate can prevent unnecessary conflict. This involves honest and open communication, timely intervention, and negotiation skills.

7.4. Emotional Intelligence: Keys to Success

Emotional intelligence is a commodity everyone should invest in, given its transformative implications on all our interpersonal interactions. Developing emotional intelligence doesn't happen overnight; it requires conscious practice, mindful engagement, and ongoing self-assessment. Yet, the benefits far outweigh the investment, especially when dealing with disagreements.

Achieving a higher level of emotional intelligence will transform the way you relate to others, better your relationships, and foster healthier environments in all aspects of your life. So embark today on this journey of self-discovery and development and witness the change in how you manage disagreements, stave off conflicts, and maintain your relationships.

Chapter 8. Building Cooperation: Collaborative Techniques for Resolving Disputes

Building cooperation is an essential facet of resolving disputes within a variety of contexts. In our lives, we often come face-to-face with situations requiring negotiation, compromise, and collaboration. The need to resolve disagreements is not just limited to our personal world but is equally intrinsic in our professional lives. Everybody, from politicians to business leaders, from teachers to parents, deals with disputes of varying scales and intensities. Effectively resolving these disputes often necessitates moving beyond individual perspectives and fostering a cooperative environment where solutions can be formulated collaboratively.

8.1. The Importance of Building Cooperation

Cooperation is instrumental in fostering an environment conducive to conflict resolution. It helps in eradicating adversarial attitudes among the parties involved, reducing the sense of rivalry and competition. The focus shifts from individual gains to a common goal, fostering a sense of unity and shared purpose. Moreover, cooperation ensures that every party's voice is heard, opinions are valued, and a harmonious relational ambience is achieved. Cooperation guarantees that not just one, but all parties involved, feel victorious once the conflict is resolved.

8.2. Understanding the Principles of Cooperation

Cooperation rests on certain fundamental principles that must be understood thoroughly.

Respect: Respect acts as the bedrock of cooperative relationships. It's about acknowledging the other parties involved as equals, valuing their perspectives, and treating them with kindness.

Mutual Understanding: Mutual understanding plays a pivotal role in cooperation. It involves clarity of communication, comprehension of the other's perspective, and finding common ground.

Patience: Patience involves giving space and time for the other party to express their thoughts, feelings, and opinions. It requires staying calm during heated moments and avoiding rash decisions.

Flexibility: Being open-minded, willing to change, and understanding that disagreements are opportunities for growth is crucial for cooperation.

Compromise: Achieving consensus requires a willingness to compromise. Parties involved must be prepared to let go of aspects of their stance for the larger good.

8.3. The Role of Communication in Building Cooperation

Effective communication forms the backbone of cooperative practices. It's not just about expressing your viewpoint eloquently but also about listening and understanding other parties' perspectives. Facilitate an open dialogue, concentrate on active listening, and be receptive to ideas. Ensure you articulate your thoughts clearly and honestly without being offensive or defensive. Good communication moves the conversation from being accusatory or confrontational to a constructive and solution-oriented direction, fostering cooperation and mutual respect.

8.4. Collaborative Techniques for Resolving Disputes

Various collaborative techniques can help build cooperation and tackle disputes effectively. These techniques provide a structured pathway for negotiation and problem-solving that ensures all parties involved feel heard, understood, and respected.

Brainstorming: Brainstorming allows for a free-flow of ideas. It encourages creativity and innovation, thereby ensuring that a wide variety of solutions are considered.

The Delphi Technique: The Delphi Technique involves using a panel of experts to gather opinions independently, aggregate the responses, and produce a decision. This method reduces bias and encourages cooperation.

Consensus Building: Consensus Building is about involving all parties in the decision-making process, fostering a sense of ownership and commitment towards the agreed solution.

Cooperative Negotiation: This technique involves focusing on interests rather than positions, creating a win-win situation rather than a zero-sum game.

8.5. The Path Forward: Turning Principles into Practice

Implementing these principles and techniques in real-life situations can truly revolutionize your approach to conflict resolution. It would involve an active effort to remain respectful and maintain open lines of communication, even in highly stressful circumstances. This course of action, although challenging at times, would invariably lead to long-lasting resolutions and harmonious relationships.

In conclusion, building cooperation is more than just a strategy for resolving disputes; it is a philosophy that enhances personal growth, mutual respect, and relational harmony. Remember, every dispute presents an opportunity to further refine these skills and contribute positively to our shared human experience.

Chapter 9. Negotiation Skills: Finding Common Ground

The tactic of negotiation is an art, a melodious symphony of words, understanding, compromise, and collaboration. This particular skill comes into play when you seek to resolve disagreements by finding common ground, a space where both parties feel heard, seen, and acknowledged. Exploring this topic in depth will require a thorough examination of negotiation strategies, the importance of being able to be flexible and adapt in contentious situations, and learning how to strike a balance between being firm in your convictions, while remaining open to different perspectives.

9.1. Understanding the Terrain

To be an effective negotiator, you need to have a sound understanding of the terrain. This involves getting a grasp on the dynamics at play in a particular disagreement. Every person involved has their own wants, needs, preferences, and biases, and these factors oftentimes contribute to the dispute. Understanding what drives people, the "why" behind their actions and statements, is key to navigating the potential minefield of disagreements. A negotiation is like a puzzle - you have to factor in all the pieces to see the whole picture.

An important aspect of understanding the terrain is identifying the underlying interests of each party. An interest can be considered the true motivation behind a person's position or argument. By uncovering these interests, it allows you to address the root of the conflict. Furthermore, understanding the emotional context of the situation is critical. Every conflict carries with it some amount of emotional baggage, which can either fuel the fire or be addressed and defused. For instance, by acknowledging emotions involved, you validate the other person's feelings, which can help minimize the emotional load and potentially reduce the intensity of the disagreement.

9.2. Building Bridges Not Walls

One widespread misconception about negotiation is that it's equivalent to a battle - a tug-of-war where one person has to win and the other loses. This win-lose perspective creates walls, not bridges. In the spirit of building bridges, negotiation is best approached as a collaborative process where both parties aim for a win-win outcome. By creating an environment of collaboration instead of competition, you minimize the likelihood of parties becoming defensive or aggressive, improving the chances of finding common ground. Prioritizing an open, respectful dialogue where everyone's input is valued and considered strengthens the relationship and ensures fairness, which promotes a more productive negotiation process.

9.3. Communicate, Don't Confront

The way you communicate during a negotiation process can either exacerbate the disagreement or navigate toward resolution. To avoid escalation, opt for non-confrontational, constructive communication. Assertive communication is key here - express your opinions clearly and emphatically, yet respectfully. Focus on "I" statements rather than "you" accusations, which can often come across as blaming or attacking. For instance, instead of saying "You never listen to me," it would be more effective to say, "I feel unheard when my points are not acknowledged."

Furthermore, active listening is a critical tool in negotiation. By really listening, you show the other party that you respect their viewpoint and that you're not just focused on pushing your agenda. Ask clarifying questions, respond reflectively, and avoid interrupting. Display open body language, maintain eye contact, and give verbal nods to show your engagement in the conversation.

9.4. Finding the Common Ground

The main goal of negotiation is to find common ground - an overlap of interests where both parties can find satisfaction. To achieve this, you need to map out a solution space where there is aligning interest. This involves brainstorming potential solutions, analyzing their implications, and progressively refining them to the best fit for everyone involved.

During this process, it's crucial to maintain an adaptable and open-minded stand. Being rigid or uncompromising can be an enemy to negotiation. In contrast, remaining flexible and open to possibilities, even those initially outside your comfort zone or expectation, can lead to innovative solutions previously unimagined. Always remember that resolution isn't about either party surrendering but about reaching an agreement that reconciles differences to the best possible extent.

9.5. Conclusion

Mastering negotiation skills is simply not an option but a necessity in order to effectively handle disagreements and find common ground. Remember, the negotiation process isn't about winning a battle or pushing an agenda; instead, it's about facilitating a fair and respectful dialogue, understanding the other party's perspective, and working collaboratively towards a win-win resolution. With patience, empathy, and skill, you can transform disagreement into an opportunity for growth, learning, and strengthened relationships.

Chapter 10. Addressing and Resolving Conflicts: Tools and Techniques

The pathway to resolving conflicts is often a winding one, filled with potential missteps and challenging interactions. This chapter lays down an array of tools and techniques that will guide you down this path with relative ease, maneuvering through this landscape with purpose and effectiveness.

10.1. Problem Identification: The First Step

Any conflict resolution begins with accurately identifying the underlying problem. It would indeed be a foolish endeavor to tread on the path of resolution without understanding the root cause of the conflict. Adopt an objective stance, putting personal biases and feelings aside to see the problem for what it truly is.

To identify a problem accurately, follow these steps:

1. Recognize there's a conflict: Acknowlegde when a disagreement has escalated into a conflict requiring resolution.
2. Define the problem: Be clear about the issue at hand. This often involves stating the problem in a simple sentence.
3. Understand everyone's interests: The interests are the needs that you want satisfied with the resolution.

Mastering this initial step is crucial in avoiding further misunderstandings and getting to the heart of a conflict.

10.2. Active Listening: A Tool for Understanding

Once you have identified the problem, the next step is active listening. It involves not just hearing the words being said but also understanding the complete message being sent. This also includes observing body language, tone, and any subtext that may be present.

Tips and techniques to enhance your active listening skills are:

1. Make eye contact: This shows the speaker that you are paying attention.
2. Don't interrupt: Let the other person say what they need to before you speak.
3. Practice empathy: Try to understand the speaker's emotions and perspectives.

Downplaying the significance of active listening in conflict resolution is a fatal error that one must strive to avoid.

10.3. Open Communication: The Bridge to Resolution

Following active listening is the need for clear, open communication. It is not just about stating facts or presenting arguments, but requires understanding, respect, patience, and control of tone and language.

To communicate effectively in conflict situations,

1. Be clear and concise: Your message should be easily understandable.
2. Focus on the issue at hand: Do not allow personal attacks or accusatory language.

3. Use "I" Statements: This helps reduce the chances of the other person feeling attacked and becoming defensive.

By following these principles of open communication, you take strides towards achieving conflict resolution with less friction and more understanding.

10.4. Conflict Styles: Understanding Your Approach

Understanding your conflict style can help you adapt your approach given the situation. The traditional conflict styles include:

1. Competing: You assert your views at the expense of others.
2. Accommodating: You yield to the other's needs, often neglecting your own.
3. Avoiding: You avoid the conflict altogether.
4. Compromising: You aim for a mutually acceptable solution.
5. Collaborating: You seek to satisfy the interests of all parties involved.

Understanding these styles can guide your response to conflict, even allowing adjustments to exacerbate a more effective resolution.

10.5. Negotiation: The Art of Agreement

Negotiation is an essential tool that aids in conflict resolution. It involves making concessions and reaching consensus for an agreement to the satisfaction of all parties involved.

Successful negotiation techniques involve:

1. Preparation: Determine what you want and what you're willing to give up.
2. Assertiveness: Express your thoughts, views and feelings in a direct but non-aggressive manner.
3. Flexibility: Be open to changes and adapt your strategy as needed.

10.6. Forgiveness and Reconciliation: The Final Steps

Once the conflict has been diligently handled, what remains is the process of forgiveness and reconciliation. This step is paramount to maintaining relationships post-conflict.

To promote forgiveness and reconciliation,

1. Express your feelings: Share how the conflict impacted you, without any blame.
2. Apologize sincerely: If you were at fault at any level, acknowledge it.
3. Accept apologies: If the other person apologizes, accept it with grace.

By fostering a forgiving environment, you allow relations to heal post-conflict, paving way for continued mutual growth and respect.

In wrapping up, it's important to note that conflict is an inescapable part of our lives, but with these tools and techniques, you can approach them with confidence and resolve them effectively. Keep honing these skills, and soon, you will master the art of conflict resolution, thereby maintaining harmony in your professional and personal relationships.

Chapter 11. Maintaining Relationships Post-Conflict: Paving Way for Forgiveness and Growth

In the aftermath of a conflict, maintaining relationships can seem to be an uphill battle. The ability to forgive, foster growth, and pave the way for reconciliation is the foundation of this resilient endeavor. Comprehending the necessity of these actions and implementing them effectively holds the key to sustainable relationships post-conflict.

11.1. The Essence of Forgiveness

Understanding the essence of forgiveness is fundamental in managing relationships after a conflict. Forgiveness is not merely a feeling; it's a conscious process wherein one decides to let go of resentment, grudges, or thoughts of revenge against someone who has caused hurt. Working through personal pain and choosing to forgive can be difficult, yet profoundly transformative.

The act of forgiveness cultivates an inner peace that pervades all aspects of life. It heralds an acceptance of personal emotions and experiences, while also acknowledging the humanity of the so-called adversary. At the core, forgiveness is a powerful testament of self-love and emotional intelligence. The ability to forgive doesn't exonerate the offender's actions, but rather it emboldens the individual to move forward without bitterness and resentment.

11.2. Reconciliation and Healing

Where forgiveness marks a personal journey of healing, reconciliation initiates a new chapter of shared growth in a relationship post-conflict. Reconciliation is, in its essence, an intentional attempt by both parties to restore the relationship and rebuild trust.

This process involves open dialogue, where each person can express their feelings, thoughts, and expectations vulnerably. Through open and honest communication, a deeper understanding is achieved, laying the foundation for mutual respect and a renewed relationship.

Furthermore, reconciliation doesn't entail returning to the previous state of the relationship as it can often be unrealistic and potentially detrimental. Rather, reconciliation involves creating a new understanding based on the lessons learned from the conflict and evolving to a healthier, more robust relationship dynamic.

11.3. Paving the Path for Post-Conflict Growth

Importantly, the aftermath of a conflict offers a fertile ground for personal and mutual growth. Recognizing conflicts as opportunities to learn optimizes the potential of post-conflict growth.

After stepping into the shoes of forgiveness and reconciliation, one naturally becomes more compassionate, empathetic, assertive, and emotionally intelligent. These experiences foster newfound knowledge on handling disagreements, managing conflict, and maintaining relationships, thereby advancing one's growth in conflict resolution skills.

Additionally, within the realm of shared growth, conflicts act as catalysts that promote deeper understanding, enhanced communication, and improved negotiation techniques. By dealing with conflicts in a proactive, constructive manner, relationships evolve to be more resilient, compassionate, and understanding.

In conclusion, maintaining relationships post-conflict is an art that requires courage, patience, and humility. Learned skills such as forgiveness, reconciliation, and fostering growth post-conflict are the pillars on which strong, lasting relationships are built. As with all learned skills, practice, open-mindedness, and willingness to change are critical to achieving success in this endeavor. A single step towards forgiveness and reconciliation can go a long way in transforming both you and your relationships, irrevocably altering your approach to conflict and disagreements. In the end, every conflict, however heated, is an opportunity for personal growth and relationship enhancement, and learning how to seize it is indeed a valuable life skill.

www.ingramcontent.com/pod-product-compliance
Lightning Source LLC
Chambersburg PA
CBHW070953220526
45471CB00007B/3010